W9-AEA-020

by Christine Peterson
illustrated by Cynthia Martin

CONSULTANT:
Michael Bailey
Colonel William J. Walsh *Associate Professor*
of American Government
Georgetown University, Washington, D.C.

Mankato, Minnesota

Graphic Library is published by Capstone Press,
151 Good Counsel Drive, P.O. Box 669, Mankato, Minnesota 56002.
www.capstonepress.com

1 2 3 4 5 6 13 12 11 10 09 08

Library of Congress Cataloging-in-Publication Data
Peterson, Christine.
 The American presidency / by Christine Peterson ; illustrated by Cynthia Martin.
 p. cm. — (Graphic library. Cartoon social studies)
 Includes bibliographical references and index.
 ISBN-13: 978-1-4296-1330-9 (hardcover)
 ISBN-10: 1-4296-1330-0 (hardcover)
 ISBN-13: 978-1-4296-1778-9 (softcover pbk.)
 ISBN-10: 1-4296-1778-0 (softcover pbk.)
 1. Presidents — United States — Juvenile literature. 2. United States — Politics and
government — Juvenile literature. I. Martin, Cynthia, 1961– II. Title. III. Series.
E176.1.P492 2008
973.09'9 — dc22   2007027341

Summary: In cartoon format, explains the history, role, and responsibilities of the president
 in United States government.

Art Director and Designer
Bob Lentz

Colorist
Michael Kelleher

Cover Artist
Kelly Brown

Editor
Christopher L. Harbo

TABLE OF CONTENTS

On a historic day in April 1789, George Washington became the first president of the United States of America. Prior to 1789, there wasn't anything like the presidency on earth.

Although the road to the presidency began at least 200 years ago, the journey continues today. More than 40 presidents have followed in Washington's footsteps.

The president is a symbol of strong national and world leadership. Every president faces joys and sorrows while in office.

No one ever said this job would be easy.

ABRAHAM LINCOLN

But all presidents come to office with a desire to serve the nation and its people.

Let's take a closer look at how the presidency began.

U.S. CONSTITUTION

The U.S. Constitution is the set of laws that govern the country. Written in 1787, the Constitution has three main parts. The preamble describes the basic ideas behind the government. The seven articles explain how the government works. The articles also say how the Constitution can be changed. The Bill of Rights is the first 10 amendments to the Constitution. These amendments guarantee basic rights to U.S. citizens.

After winning the Revolutionary War with Britain in 1783, the United States was in trouble. Farmers and officials clashed over taxes. States had different laws and money. The nation's government was bruised and almost broken.

BENJAMIN FRANKLIN 👉

In 1787, leaders from the 13 states held a Constitutional Convention in Philadelphia to fix the national government. Some delegates favored the old government under the **Articles of Confederation.** This document provided for a weak national government, and gave states the power to set taxes and call out troops. Other delegates wanted to junk the Articles and create a new national government.

Articles of Confederation — the original set of laws governing the 13 American Colonies during the Revolutionary War

Virginia delegate James Madison was a small man with big ideas. Madison created a new government with three parts called branches.

Delegates wanted a new kind of leader for the executive branch. They didn't want one person to have too much power like Britain's King George. Colonists had just fought to be free of him. Delegates decided that a president should serve the people — and answer to them as well.

CHECKS AND BALANCES

The U.S. government has a system of checks and balances. No one branch has more power than the other. The president must approve laws passed by the legislative branch. The judicial branch makes sure laws don't conflict with the Constitution. Senators must okay the president's choices for the Supreme Court.

Presidents and their Cabinets lead the executive branch of government.

Hey, watch it, pal. Make room in the Cabinet for me.

But this cabinet isn't a wooden box where you store cups and plates.

Instead, the president's Cabinet is a group of leaders who help make decisions for the country. Cabinet members also lead different departments within the government.

We have no time for such foolishness.

We've got a country to run.

ORDER OF SUCCESSION

When a president dies or leaves office unexpectedly, a line of people is ready to take the job.

Looks like we're going to have a long wait in line.

NOW PLAYING: THE PRESIDENCY

First in line is the vice president. If he or she is unable to serve, the Speaker of the House gets the job. In all, 18 cabinet members and other officials are in line to become president, if needed.

At meetings, 15 Cabinet members and the vice president gather around a long oval desk. These leaders give the president advice on issues facing the country.

This group plans ways to keep our country safe and how best to spend government money. Cabinet members also give the president advice on the military, law enforcement, and transportation.

A PRESIDENT'S JOB

A president's job description is short, but full of responsibilities.

THOMAS JEFFERSON

The president's number one job is to lead the country. That means putting the needs of the people and the country first.

This job won't leave much time for farming or anything else.

Presidents have powers and responsibilities to help them serve the nation. They can appoint people to lead government departments or serve on the Supreme Court. Congress, however, must approve some of the president's choices.

Congress rejected my choice for the courts.

That's checks and balances for you, Mr. President.

Presidents can also suggest ideas for new laws. But a member of Congress must introduce the **bill** for a vote.

I'm going to introduce you to some friends.

Thanks for thinking of me, Mr. President.

bill — a written plan for a new law that is discussed and voted on for approval

Congress passes bills and the president signs them into law. Sometimes presidents use their veto power. It's not exactly a super-power, but a veto can stop a bill from becoming law.

GROVER CLEVELAND

Ahhh. You got me!

Presidents can veto bills they believe are weak or not in the country's best interest. Vetoed bills must go back to Congress for changes.

RONALD REAGAN

You need work, partner.

If Congress disagrees with the president's veto, lawmakers can vote on the bill again. Congress can override a veto if two-thirds of its members vote in favor of the bill. If the bill doesn't win two-thirds of the vote, it is considered dead.

VETO MANIACS

Presidents Franklin Roosevelt and Grover Cleveland top the list of presidents with the most vetoes. Roosevelt issued 372 vetoes. Cleveland issued 304.

The president is often called the commander-in-chief. That's because the president is in charge of the U.S. military. The president has the power to order military troops into battle when needed.

But it's also important for presidents to cooperate with other countries. Presidents often meet with leaders of foreign countries to talk about world peace, trade, military strategy, and other issues. Presidents also work out treaties with other nations.

PAY DAY

For all this work, presidents are paid $400,000 a year. Most pro baseball players, however, earn about $2.4 million a year.

And though it's not part of the job description, presidents must be good communicators. They can't be shy or hide from the people. It's important for presidents to clearly tell citizens about their plans and decisions.

IMPEACHMENT

Presidents must be honest with the people they serve. Some presidents, however, haven't done a great job. When a president breaks a law, Congress can vote to impeach the president. Impeachment is rare. Andrew Johnson and Bill Clinton were brought up on impeachment charges. Both impeachments failed and both men remained in office.

A PRESIDENT'S DAY

Rise and shine, Mr. President. It's time to start your day. There's little time to sleep, if you're the leader of a country.

Mornings mean meetings in the Oval Office. Big meetings. Small meetings. Presidents attend them all. They may meet with an **ambassador** from a different country to discuss trade deals.

ambassador — a person sent by a government to represent it in another country

Advisors come and go from the Oval Office with news on bills, treaties, and other issues.

At the Capitol, the president meets with lawmakers about taxes or health care.

Then it's back to the Oval Office.

Finally, some time for myself.

Well, not exactly. Presidents usually have a pile of papers to sort through. They must read speeches, reports from Cabinet members, treaties, bills, and letters from citizens like you. Presidents also spend a lot of time talking on the phone.

THE SECRET IS OUT

SECRET SERVICE AGENTS

The president is followed wherever he goes by a group of skilled agents. These men and women make up the Secret Service. This agency is best known for keeping the president, vice president, and their families safe.

The president's job often must be done far away from home. Presidents travel throughout the country and around the world to meet with other leaders or U.S. soldiers. The president logs thousands of miles each year by car, helicopter, and plane.

AIR FORCE ONE

If you want to become president, you have to follow some rules.

RULES FOR U.S. PRESIDENT:

MUST BE A NATURAL BORN CITIZEN.

MUST HAVE LIVED IN THE UNITED STATES FOR AT LEAST 14 YEARS.

MUST BE AT LEAST 35 YEARS OLD.

Pay attention. These rules haven't been broken in more than 200 years.

Today, U.S. presidents serve four-year terms. They can serve two terms for a total of eight years in office.

DWIGHT EISENHOWER

THOMAS JEFFERSON

JIMMY CARTER

RONALD REAGAN

Before leading the nation, presidents held other jobs. They served as governors, senators, and representatives. Some were famous war generals. Fourteen U.S. presidents worked as lawyers. A few presidents worked as teachers and farmers. One was even an actor!

Most presidents had excellent educations. But not Abraham Lincoln. He had less than a year of formal education. But he made up for it with natural smarts.

I'm a quick study too.

Family ties can also lead someone to the presidency. John Quincy Adams became president 28 years after his father, John Adams, held the office. William Henry Harrison and his grandson Benjamin both held the nation's top job.

Presidents Theodore Roosevelt and Franklin Roosevelt were distant cousins. George H. W. Bush and his son, George W., are another father-son duo who both served as president.

SIZE DOESN'T MATTER

Tall, short, fat, and skinny, presidents come in all shapes and sizes. Abraham Lincoln was the tallest president at 6 feet 4 inches. James Madison was the shortest man to hold office at just 5 feet 4 inches tall.

Presidential candidates belong to political parties.

No. Not that kind of a party.

I just love parties. Where's the cake?

ANDREW JACKSON

You mean there's not going to be any cake?

Political parties choose candidates to run for public offices. Each political group believes their ideas are best for the country. Candidates and party members spend millions of dollars to inform people about their plans for the country.

Ooh, Ooh. Pick me. Pick me.

The Democrats and Republicans are the two largest political parties in the United States. But smaller third parties also nominate candidates to run for president.

Somebody has to clean up the mess these two make.

3RD PARTY

Months before the presidential election, party members gather at large conventions. Conventions might look like pep rallies, but they are serious work. Party delegates must choose a candidate for president.

Politicians make lots of speeches at conventions as members build the party's platform of ideas and goals. Each plank in a platform stands for an idea the party believes will help the country.

As your candidate, I promise you'll never have to eat broccoli again!

After the platform is complete, delegates must choose candidates for president and vice president. They vote for candidates they believe will best serve the country. Candidates represent the party and its platform of ideas in the presidential election.

After the convention, it's time to hit the campaign trail. Presidential candidates race across the country sharing their ideas with the people.

In years past, candidates traveled on horseback or on foot to deliver their campaign messages.

What's your rush? The election is months away!

Trains and planes allowed candidates to cover more miles during the campaign.

HARRY S. TRUMAN EXPRESS

Vote for MMMEEEEEEEEE!

As technology changed, so did presidential campaigns. After 1960, televised debates became a popular campaign tool.

In November, the power lies with the voters. Every four years, U.S. citizens cast their votes for president. Elections are held on the Tuesday after the first Monday in November.

ELECTION OF 1800

In 1800, Thomas Jefferson became the third president of the United States after an odd election. After votes were cast, Jefferson was tied with Aaron Burr for the presidency. Congress was asked to break the tie. After 26 rounds of voting in Congress, Jefferson won the presidency.

So, the candidate with the most votes gets to be president, right? Well, not really.

You've got to be kidding me! How can that be?

Back in 1787, the Founding Fathers didn't want to leave such an important decision to the people. But they didn't want Congress in charge of selecting the president, either. That's why they formed the Electoral College.

Never heard of this college? It's not a school but a small group of state representatives who have the final say in electing our president. Electoral College members vote for the candidate who received the most popular votes in their home state.

I can't wait to represent the people back home.

But the candidate with the most popular votes doesn't always win. Here's why. States with large populations have more electoral votes than states with fewer residents. A candidate may win the popular vote in some states but lose the presidency at the Electoral College. To become president, a candidate must receive at least 270 of the 538 electoral votes.

ELECTION OF 2000

In the presidential election of 2000, Democratic candidate Al Gore received about 500,000 more popular votes than Republican George Bush. But Gore lost the presidency in the Electoral College. George Bush carried the Electoral College with 271 votes to become the country's 43rd president.

After the election results are finalized, the country prepares for inauguration day. On this day, the president officially begins a new term in office.

I do solemnly swear . . .

Since 1938, presidents have been sworn into office on January 20. It is a day of speeches, parades, and glamorous dances.

Come on, Mary. Let's boogie!

But on inauguration day, no words are more important than the ones taken right from the Constitution.

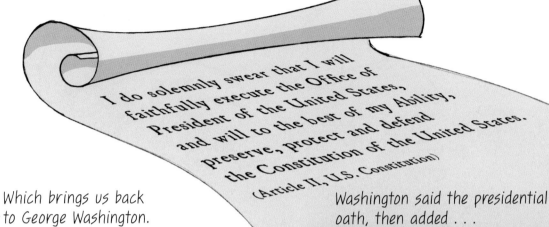

I do solemnly swear that I will faithfully execute the Office of President of the United States, and will to the best of my Ability, preserve, protect and defend the Constitution of the United States.

(Article II, U.S. Constitution)

Which brings us back to George Washington.

Washington said the presidential oath, then added . . .

I thought you had forgotten about me.

So help me God.

To this day, every president has said these same words at their inaugurations.

This oath has guided presidents as they take on one of the most difficult jobs in the world.

Difficult, yes, but there is no greater job in the land.

Time Line

April 10, 1789 — George Washington becomes the first president of the United States. Leaders from the 13 states unanimously choose Washington to lead the new nation.

April 10, 1789

April 30, 1803 — Thomas Jefferson doubles the size of the United States by signing the Louisiana Purchase. The area includes what is now Louisiana, Arkansas, Oklahoma, Missouri, Kansas, Colorado, Iowa, South Dakota, North Dakota, Minnesota, Wyoming, and Montana.

April 30, 1803

November 7, 1944 — Franklin Delano Roosevelt becomes the only president elected to four terms in office. In 1951, the 22nd Amendment to the Constitution limits presidents to just two terms in office.

November 7, 1944

November 22, 1963 — A gunman kills President John F. Kennedy in Dallas, Texas. Kennedy is shot as his car travels along Dallas streets lined with thousands of people.

November 22, 1963

July 2, 1964 — President Lyndon Johnson signs the Civil Rights Act. This law ends segregation and guarantees equal rights to all Americans.

July 2, 1964

August 15, 1814 — British troops invade Washington, D.C., and burn the White House. First Lady Dolley Madison manages to save several historic paintings as she flees the mansion.

November 19, 1863 — President Abraham Lincoln delivers his Gettysburg Address. Lincoln's speech is just 265 words, but is considered one of the greatest presidential speeches ever made.

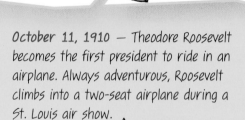

AUGUST 15, 1814

October 11, 1910 — Theodore Roosevelt becomes the first president to ride in an airplane. Always adventurous, Roosevelt climbs into a two-seat airplane during a St. Louis air show.

NOVEMBER 19, 1863

OCTOBER 11, 1910

August 9, 1974 — Richard Nixon becomes the first U.S. president to resign from office. Nixon leaves office following the Watergate scandal.

November 7, 2000 — George W. Bush wins one of the closest presidential elections in history. Bush loses the popular vote but wins more ballots in the Electoral College.

AUGUST 9, 1974

NOVEMBER 7, 2000

GLOSSARY

ambassador (am-BASS-uh-dur) — a person sent by a government to represent it in another country

Articles of Confederation (AR-ti-kuhls UHV kuhn-fed-er-AY-shun) — the original set of laws governing the 13 American Colonies during the Revolutionary War

bill (BIL) — a written plan for a new law that is discussed and voted on for approval or disapproval

campaign (kam-PAYN) — to try to gain support from people in order to win an election

constitution (kon-stuh-TOO-shuhn) — the system of laws that state the rights of the people and the powers of the government

delegate (DEL-uh-guht) — person chosen to speak and act for others

Electoral College (ee-lehk-TOHR-uhl KAHL-uhj) — the group of people that elects the president and vice president after the general election

impeach (im-PEECH) — to bring formal charges against a public official who may have committed a crime while in office

inauguration (i-NAW-gyur-ray-shun) — the ceremony in which the president of a country is installed in office

succession (suhk-SEH-shuhn) — the order in which people replace someone who has left a position

veto (VEE-toh) — the power or right to stop a bill from becoming law

West Wing (WEST WING) — a section of the White House that includes dozens of offices for the press and the president's staff

READ MORE

Egan, Tracie. *The President and the Executive Branch*. A Primary Source Library of American Citizenship. New York: Rosen, 2004.

Fradin, Dennis B. *The U.S. Constitution*. Turning Points in U.S. History. New York: Marshall Cavendish Benchmark, 2007.

Hamilton, John. *Branches of Government*. Government in Action! Edina, Minn.: ABDO, 2005.

Hempstead, Anne. *The White House*. Land of the Free. Chicago: Heinemann, 2006.

St. George, Judith. *So You Want to be President?* New York: Philomel Books, 2004.

INTERNET SITES

FactHound offers a safe, fun way to find Internet sites related to this book. All of the sites on FactHound have been researched by our staff.

Here's how:
1. Visit www.facthound.com
2. Choose your grade level.
3. Type in this book ID 1429613300 for age-appropriate sites. You may also browse subjects by clicking on letters, or by clicking on pictures and words.
4. Click on the Fetch It button.

FactHound will fetch the best sites for you!

INDEX